the sweet fuels

Erin Knight

the sweet fuels

for Naomi
so good to see
you again

Hugs,
E~ Kf.

July 2007.

Cover photo by Jason Verschoor, istockphoto.com.
Cover and interior page design by Julie Scriver.
Printed in Canada.
10 9 8 7 6 5 4 3 2 1

Library and Archives Canada Cataloguing in Publication

Knight, Erin, 1980-
    The sweet fuels / Erin Knight.

Poems.
Includes bibliographical references.
ISBN 978-0-86492-491-9
    I. Title.

PS8621.N54S94 2007   C811'.6   C2007-900407-5

Goose Lane Editions acknowledges the financial support of the Canada Council for the Arts, the Government of Canada through the Book Publishing Industry Development Program (BPIDP), and the New Brunswick Department of Wellness, Culture and Sport for its publishing activities.

Goose Lane Editions
Suite 330, 500 Beaverbrook Court
Fredericton, New Brunswick
CANADA E3B 5X4
www.gooselane.com

for Grandad
Andrew Jerome Jones
1926-2006

Contents

Part I

Sound Travels Light

End of a healing summer,
you stand at a lakeshore, a fish
has leapt just outside your view.
A fish leaps — you know by
knowing the sound of water
closing over the body.

Did I really say *end of a healing*?

The spent blood returns
to the heart, a kind governance.
I will never stop wondering
at the strength of the call
to travel home. End of season,
two fingers at your wrist.
The first snow will be difficult
to distinguish from rain.

The Sight

Some children and corvids have it.
Women who lived by the sea were often
touched by it, not without consequence.
But you get by on a few good sleeps,
heavy snowfall warnings and a healthy fear
of inertia. There's the reassuring
geometry of the calendar on the wall,
and opportunity to trust the stranger
who sells you unpasteurized brie —
which is not the same trust as you have
in the meter reader, who disappears
into your basement to record how much
energy you've spent, and if you never
let him in he relies on the law of averages —
what does he discover in the furnace rooms
of the neighbourhood, descending daily
humanity's dark stairs? Nobody
with the sight is ever envied, one blue egg
among three or four mottled green.
Now the days are getting shorter so surely
someone is seeing to the end of them,
and the crows amass in a collective
ecstasy of unease at every early dusk.
You're keeping calm. Now and then,
you pick up the phone, restore it to its cradle
again. The dial tone an acquired comfort,
like sweet cheese, or the smell of burning dust
when you turn on the furnace the first day.

Secondary Highway

Take the small maps on your knees. Grasses
traced routes there as you took back your wind,
while backstory spun in the bicycle tires.
When you stand, can you still read the legend
creased in the skin, is this your quietest scar?

In the flat heat of noon you have nothing.
Just thirst, which is ancient, a deer's jawbone
caked in the creekbed. Before noon had a name
sun crested each day; dry-thoated, you remember.
A question taut in your muscle: *how much longer.*

If only every departure had the weighted corners
of this sky, one-eyed blue: your dog Loki,
his injury of blindness. A car hit him once
and he kept on running; a year later, hit again.
At the highway's shoulder, you found him.

All witness is through angles: the hawk's dive,
bent stems, and the toothed oil from the chain
at your calf. Your skin still spending salt
from reserves you've emptied. Where loneliness
stretches to the convex lens of the sky,

these yellow fields will leach you or unburden,
you might look at the pothole that threw you
and feel asphalt knows something of memory.
It's water, freezing through winter; the strength
in that stillness breaks open the road.

Leduc #2

Then there is so much you open your arms.

Outstretched, they grow so heavy.
If that weight were measured
it would be in stone — and even this
inaccurate. Because west of the Shield
stone means transience: the river valley claims
another house each spring,
while further south, cottonwoods
strangle their own tallest limbs and the wind strips
another sheet of sandstone.

There's no patience here, and
why would there be — a horizon you want to run towards
until a bone splinters in your heel, no wonder
this prairie tries to stare down finity.
Its black soil, even blacker veins.
You saw a boy once
break his collarbone doing stunts
off the ridge, and his anger, I'm *fine,*
while the keel inside him shifted —

Meanwhile: your open arms.
Your unbroken view, and the city
at your back, its adolescent sinew.

The Red Belt

A weather that is unusual and unpredictable makes people
distrust each other; they become obsessed with the new,
because they have to give up their habits. That is why
despots like all areas where the weather is moral.
— Friedrich Nietzsche

This is not a wise place in which to lay your trust.
The snow can disappear without ever being seen
to melt, weeks of ice sublimate in an hour and rob
lakes of volume. The white birch predictably die.

Most of us walk through the days with a scratch
in the throat. It's not always caused by a germ
or the threat of tears. The package should be here
in a week, but a week can mean a difference

of forty degrees Celsius, and it's not just the winds
that change. A chinook brings extreme dryness.
The Red Belt is a crescent of rust-coloured pines
dehydrated by irregular warmth; the needles

release moisture to the balmy air but the roots
find nothing to take. All restlessness stirred.
Sound stirred, and driven over great distance
as if carried across water. On those open days

when the chinook arch borders an emptied sky,
a log might be split with the wind's arid weight.
And you had thought you were alone.
You catch a shock, crossing the carpet to the door.

Regionalism

I considered laying my dying goldfish on a bed of ice in the deep freeze. To give the slow sleep and to soothe its rotting fins, the small pustules at the gills. My mother told me I should be more realistic. Of course I knew how cold burns. But with purpose. Instead she wrapped the goldfish in tinfoil and brought a brick down over its body in the driveway. It was a quick death. I found that I was compelled to look inside the aluminum shroud: mercy was all gold and reds, flecks of silver. I had not known that *colour* could be plural in the way that *moose* and *deer* are, multiplied afterthoughts of the Trans-Canada Highway. My mother said that's because I'd never seen an eastern fall. I wondered where she had found the brick. Out here the decade of stucco and red shag has never passed.

Cast Your Own Shadow at the Sixth Hour

The Romans agreed that only one hour
was ever fixed: when the sun reached its zenith
in the sky. If you want to meet me, meet me
then. The rest of the day will fall to either side,
and when, in winter, the sun only rises
to our chests, we will not ask, *is this all there is?*
The place doesn't matter. And if there is wind,
the ravine will offer low-ground shelter
from the chill. At the sixth hour our bodies
will be the pendulum of the swung day;
we'll discuss summer, the back roads, cow parsnip
the size of us. Remember weeks when the plain
was washed with a primary palette and noon
suspended us, shadowless, dry-mouthed.

The Lesser Vowel Shift

I want you to spell my name differently
every day. I believe I can ask this of you
because we haven't expected enough
of the silent letters in our language.
There's a gnosis in the undersides of leaves,
silver edges turned up before a storm.
We could wait with such reverence.
On the last day of spring snow
and klister, we scored rills in our skis
to streamline the water our movements
would melt. What if we could remember
the small animal prints we tracked
in each letter, when they were still glyphs
above our fingertips and we mouthed
every word? What if our memory
of the difference between breathe
and breathing were photographic?
Not to lose the little *e* — a chipped tooth
in a cup of milk — but to hold every vowel,
this tongue's history, the winter there.
Use letters that say nothing but *give, rest,*
and wait for me, back at the run-off.

Old Route Secondary (off Hwy 529)

I guess we've come all this way knowing so little.
Every mineral owns its own gravity.
Large landscapes pull with this cumulative
strength. *A natural tendency, the effect of this,*
especially the falling of bodies to the earth.
Such a passive theory, but beautiful
as most of them are. The fibres around here
resist touch — bullrush caked with grit,
the blade of quackgrass I split with sound,
your palm when it's cracked with winter.
The road when it cracks with winter.
Before the highway was rerouted, weeds
broke through the asphalt and began to take it back.
Soon, a cartographer will take it off the map.

Little Brown Bat

Once, my brother brought home a bat that had a wooden
peg punched through both wings, nailing them together
as if in prayer. What could I do? I held the other end of
the rope of a small person's panic, and though I was a small
person too, it had been given to me, this end, because I was
the stronger.

I found I had a voice like my mother's. I said, "Put it in
a box and put this towel over top." (I had the idea that
suffering deserved darkness, enclosed space, and the faint,
damp smell of terry cloth). I stood on a kitchen chair to
reach the phone book. Why had I never felt closer — to my
brother, to some kind of affirmation — when everything I
did was false? The woman at the SPCA asked me if I could
bring in the bat. "No," I said, "I am only eight."

At times I've been reminded of the bat's naked wings.
The skin stretched across its long fingerbones invites the
violence of an archaic past we don't claim. It must echo
with something in ourselves: maybe the folds that hang
from our upper arms when we shed muscle, or loose jowls.
One evening I overheard a woman say that memory is just
something the dead are shouting at us. What would this
sound like? November, four thousand bats asleep in a cave.
If they are startled, they starve by spring.

Shin Splint

1.

The runner's heel makes 900 strikes against the earth
every kilometre. That's cadence with a force
four times the weight of the body, the bass line
that drives the beat, then overtakes the song —

2.

Now how to love stillness when it's the shin's
lost confidence, poor bone a latchkey kid who sits
in terror on his mother's bed until her key turns
the lock at five, and the house becomes human again?

3.

Healing is the recovery of time. The fibres in the leg
recast dropped stitches, a woman in the corner stays up
darning socks. A train whistles. The mail has come.
Muscle to tendon to bone, soft beat: *Leg, love, dear one.*

Airborne

The first bakers had more faith. They knew night air
to be generous; it filled the mouths of their sleeping children
and then some. Breeze was an ingredient,

catch the breeze an invocation. The dough in the window
      would rise
or it wouldn't, depending on the histories of the air currents,
where they'd been hours before, if they carried yeast.

The baker's son dreamed of being airborne. Whenever he stood
at the edge of something (Earth's surface, his mother's roof,
the high plateaus to the south), he imagined leaping into flight.

It can't be that much harder than leavening, he thought,
and dough would rise most of the time. His chest rose
as he drew a long breath. The wind picked up.

Last week, three in the morning, I was driving home after
we ended things for good. I didn't get far. I pulled over,
and it happened I stopped curb-side of the bakery down
      the street.

The lights were out but every window open, pats of dough
on trolleys pushed up against the walls. When, one day, a batch
had risen to twice its size, the first bakers set aside a piece

and kept it as they did the home hearth fire. Sourdough
is still made with this recipe, the ferment of memory, cool air
warming over unbaked bread at forsaken hours, and rising.

Sweet Fuels

Many days of winter now,
sweet fuels crystallize.
Honey and jams lose their
liquid clarity. After this

I think the sunlight
is precipitate: grit, and knots
of ice borne by wind. It strikes
what phantom leaves still hold,
bleached to transparency.
Hands of a woman who has outlived
everyone she ever loved.

On the day I was stillest
you told me, in honey
there is a dispensable light.
That I should take spoonfuls
medicinally. But sweetness
catches in the throat.

What am I afraid of? That ritual
is what makes the day pass.
I pour boiling water into my cup.
I stir a honeyed spoon
until the crystals dissolve.
With the same motion,
I twisted a last stem
from the branch.
Thin wrists.

Mohs Hardness Scale

Talc   (scratched by a fingernail)

Humidity: skin on my skin, the heat
eliminates each morning. Guitar's
out of tune, I can't close the door, warped wood
and warped covers of books. (Do you remember
the air of sage and sand and burnt kindling,
our ears and our fingernails filling with dust?
When it was dryness that chafed
and not us, one last imported peach
that never ripened, insistent hardness
of a fruit picked green, its split stone?)

To perfectly cleave. The pared moon
a pale scratch on the sky. Air against
the skin seldom corresponds
to what the thermometer reads.
Obsolete mercury. Mercurial body.

Calcite   (scratched by a copper coin)

Copper coin, small weapon, my father's
superstition, *find a penny give a penny*,
he gave me every one he found.
Give a penny if you give a knife
to a friend — you need something,
in parting, to dull the sharp edge.

I've never received a letter I read
only once. Your handwritten words
repeated as if read through spar,
dullest crystal — I'd never been so aware
of how volatile ink and leaves and rock
can be: green tinge of corrosion
on the roofs, colour of age, of limestone lakes;
I was running out of money, the old saying,
write if you get work —

Fluorite   (scratched by a knife blade or window glass)

That a bone in your foot cracked
and healed in my absence.
Absence like a room
I had entered, four walls
and a jammed door, the site at which
so much happens: *in,* in my absence.
I saw a boy on the bus with his arm in a cast,
the bone healing, surely healing, and
it filled me with a kind of joy.

Four walls. A window for looking out
of my absence. That image of a palm
against the pane, scratched by window glass
or a knife blade, how in this test
these two are equated: a knife,
a window for looking out.

Feldspar   (scratches a knife blade or window glass)

I needed to go whatever distance
it would take to escape the grating
against the windowpane. There's violence
in the motor idling on a snowed-in street,
the vitreous morning so breakable.
If sound is the moving of waves
then silence is what draws in their tide,
lustre of moonstone: it's the imperfections
capture the light, the palm print
on the kaolin vase that recalls
the rotation of the potter's wheel.

There was a place we came to one day
where I was sure every noise had run to,
and finally stopped. Sound stunned
for a moment, granite shore.

Diamond   (scratches all common materials)

Why write only *if*? Why not write if sunlight
strikes the dust motes in the room, if a splinter
wedges beneath your nail, if you fall
in love, if you fall? Write the nub of graphite
in your palm, pure carbon, memory
of a long-ago word — so many of us have it
lodged beneath the skin, and the healing
is the having made it a part of us.

A dull mineral can be cut for fire
and brilliance, the cut brings out the light.
It's a difficult craft; more difficult is attending
to the shavings lost when the cuts are made.
Flecks of gold, pine-sharp sawdust, questions
asked by letter and forgotten, never answered.
This is the hardest substance known.

Fenester

I was told I would get my bearings soon.
I wondered when these would be given to me.

All I wanted was a perch at the best window
to watch the snowfall. *Which is the best window?*

The one that wants to be larger. *Don't they all?*
Not true. Some never imagine the other exposures.

The best window welcomes shifting angles
of light and so, in its window way, time-zones.

It knows there are those to the north and the west
and that its day has started without them. *Oh,*

said this other voice, who was really my divided self
created from a specified loneliness held in abeyance,

and who had already taken a perch at the best window
from which to watch the snowfall: *as did mine.*

Trinity of the Ear

In the ear we find shapes
of great mythologies.
First, a small shell.
Cambrian scribe.
Treasure of architecture; a structure
that circulates memory
of the ocean's depth; waves
and balanced tides.
A cathedral to house
the highest devotion:
la Sagrada Familia; tympanic
ceiling of the Opera House
or the tide pool at which a child
crouches, head bent
over the intermittent lives
of mollusks, wet sand.

Second, the labyrinth.
A name given to confess
we do not wholly understand.
In the labyrinth, sight
means very little. Orientation
depends on small hairs
bowing down within the ear.
Maze-like patterns on the floors
of medieval churches
reminded the congregation that to be lost
has been requisite for salvation
since the first garden was barred.
Not every labyrinth
is purgatory. Children run
towards the open entrance

of a maze of corn, lovers
in Victorian novels lose themselves
between hedgerows,
and the old gardener alone
remembers the map.
Desire to abandon
the other senses and rely,
for a moment completely,
on the quiet, pious hairs of the ear.
They kneel at their tiny altar,
gifts of golden string.

Third, a city of canals.
Bárány examined the inner ear
and found a maze of alleyways
filled with ever tilting fluid.
As tourists we're drawn
to old cities at sea level
or better yet, below — New Orleans,
Venice, Delft — where millers
and thieves and the holy
float on gondolas and punts.
What goes on within the canals
is dependent on inertia.
Lapse gives us our bearings:
when the gondelier turns
yet another blind corner
or stops short, driving
the oar into the ground,
our bodies move but the fluid
in the ear lags behind.

The Good Host

Anciently, when the poets came to dinner
loaves of bread were baked in the shape of the lyre.

Wine jugs and mugs were ornamented with writing.
Among the earliest examples of the alphabet

is an invitation: *Whoever drinks from this cup
swiftly will the desire of fair-crowned Aphrodite*

seize him. Then the Romans turned their attention
to wheat, and ten hundred thousand nomads

stopped wandering. It came to pass in those days
that a son was born in the city of bread.

He would later spend a night in a garden called
oil press. He had a cup that was unadorned.

The Good Hostess

On the first day
you make a sourdough.
The following day,
make two sponges:
beat and beat until
the arm rebels.
Use only one hand.
Do not try to release it
from the dough.
Keep picking up
as much as will adhere
and throw it back
hard with a turn
of the wrist.
This is repeated
about fifty times.
By then the dough
should be glistening smooth
and your fingers
will have become free.
(For a long time now,
she has equated bread
with the body.)

Part II

The Muscle Mourns its Minerals

Now that nights left are numbered I wake to my seized calf,
fist in the muscle worrying through darkness. Distilled heat,
silt over my skin and rills of insomnia through my pores.
Listen: the muscular scream, involuntary contractions
of time a tied knot so I remember how at first lacking autumn
I couldn't sleep either: the unlockable door to the open

film of curtains articulating air currents, anticipating
midnight torrents in the morning my sock feet
finding rain on linoleum, still dusk. I waited for the hour
when sky met the blue shade of leaf-flowers, wall climbing:
this was when I chose to run, always ignoring thirst.
I found a man on the sun side of the driest hill

where the only cactus had been carved with names *(te amo)*,
he crouched there each morning, inhaling roan breath
of desert, his calves near the dust — so close are the places
we imagine we're returning when the senses deceive.
I called this man *homesick*; salt thinned from my body;
once in the shade I smelled cold green growth, believed

without thinking these were the first shoots of Alberta rose,
the scent spring — next few strides I didn't know where I was.
I stored these slight impacts in my muscle soleus, waking
burn of the sun and sweat minerals that dissolve to ache —
out of sleep I'm asking what it takes to open the eyes
of a spasm because thirst, this arching foot, it isn't mine.

El gallo en el balcón
Elva Macías

Un gallo duerme en el balcón,
mi hija lo cuida en las mañanas.
Y en la noche,
cuando el poeta canta
de cómo una llama que flota entre los dos
es sólo una palabra,
el gallo anuncia
una y otra y otra vez mi traición.

The Rooster on the Balcony

Elva Macías

A rooster sleeps on the balcony,
my daughter tends to him each morning.
And in the evening,
when the poet sings
of how the flame that floats between them
is nothing but a word, once
and again and again the rooster
announces my betrayal.

Waters That Are Also Holy (I)

Gabriela believed in the holiness of water.
In the aqueous state of grace. After boiling eggs
she would cool the water in a tall clay pitcher
and set it on the table for us to drink. She believed
the calcium suspended there would be enough
to strengthen us, to keep our egg teeth
from snapping off so young.

Señora Gabriela was not really my mother
but there is no other word
for the woman who broke raw eggs into sweet milk
to spoon me, when I had been weakened
by unfamiliar water. A yolk glaze dripped
from her whisk to the green and mustard
flower printed counter. Years passed.
What this means is there came a morning
when my mother Gabriela found I daily
poured water down the drain after boiling,
for as long as I'd been lighting the stove.
She had warned me of its unpredictable
flame, she wore a scar at her naked eyebrow.
I would strike matches only for their phosphorous
hiss, but I didn't confess to this as well.

My mother had never heard of an egg timer,
but she imagined the globe milk of a yolk
closing like the second lid of a snake eye.
And she knew there is always loss
in the phase change, her arthritic knuckles
growing solid from the joint core out. Energy
in forms other than light — like the daughters

they named after her: *Gabriela, Gabriela, Gabriela;*
children of three broken-hearted men who went years
before speaking her name again.

She would make a cake called *tres leches,* three milks,
so white and wet it's like sweetened cream, but risen.
We were baking together, and when we found a yolk
tinted with blood, she spilled the batter
at the roots of the avocado.
It was the first time I saw her throw anything out.
When I remember Gabriela, I know strength
must be stolen. In the kitchen, eleven eggs
were absorbing all the new heat the air could offer.

Other Holy Waters (II)

                    Steam burns by taking
the coolness of the skin as currency. When it got me
at the forearm I dropped the colander into the sink
and the spaghetti writhed with the freedom of being,
for a moment, forgotten. The return to fluency
is not always gentle. My wrist responded
with water of its own, a supple blister, small sun.

I didn't know what to do with this new coin.
I supposed I should find a cream or salve
but instead I found comfort in the egg-shaped
evidence, mark of exchange — marketplace
of heat, and its consequence, and coolness,
and its consequence. I wanted to go back then,
to try remembering what happens during the wait
for the blister to form. Once, I blistered my tongue
on hot milk and Señora Gabi told me I had been saved
from saying something I would regret. Might
have been blasphemy, or a profession of love;
it depended on where the tongue was burned:
the part for bitter, the part for sweet.

Sometimes I think the walls might come down
and I wouldn't respond, the extent of my lassitude.
But the body takes care of that: reflex arc,
sweep from nerve to muscle, a spectrum of light
so complete it's like pain, might as well be.
The arc the shortcut to reaction, to presence,
to getting your priorities straight. It's knowing,

for once and without question, what to do
when it all goes wrong: *one*, take away your hand,
two, call on adrenalin, fluid in the bloodstream, and pain
that is simple: like this, the burn on my arm.
I know what caused it, *heat*; I know to soothe it,
ice; I know what heals: the warmth of living,
the coolness of sleep, gradual flux of day to day.

It's so dry here. When I was a child, my mother
washed my hair in canola oil because my scalp
came apart in flakes. Yesterday I let a pot boil dry
to give moisture to the room and fill the window
with steam. To add something to the condensation
on the glass, not just this small cloud of breath,
my forehead against the cold pane.

Milk-Holy Waters (III)

A recipe. If return were this simple.
The idea is that there are steps you can follow
to recreate the same flavour, texture, and
sometimes the warmth again. What you need
is a number of ingredients in their genuine
forms and a certain, specified heat.
People say, *this was my grandmother's recipe,*
and it means a net was swept through the air
after a young woman arrived in a new country,
and the senses were caught there and brought
forward for good. Sense of taste, smell,
and sight, the thin wings of insects: that's why
we waft a scent towards the face, wave
our hands over the mouth when we burn
the tongue, why we blink.

The recipe I found, years after coming back,
called for cubes of bread soaked in milk.
Might as well be a recipe for convalescence:
the body sealing together like the skin
over cream. I have never nursed a baby bird,
but if I did I might stupidly use this recipe
because milk heals you by taking you home.
I remember the taste of my mother's milk:
slightly blue and sweet, temperature of her body.
I remember holding it in my cheeks for as long
as I could while I stared out the backyard window
with my back to her. It was snowing.

Scalded milk. The yolk of an egg. Yeast
in warm water. Kneading. We had a blue bowl
I would cover with a tea towel, my mother put it atop
the fridge, and the dough was given an afternoon
to double. Odour of doubling. Insects at the screen.
What is it that goes wrong when a recipe fails,
when the dough is stiff and flat or the cake
won't set? It's like sitting in a chair, your hands
folded in your lap; it's the moment before standing
that drags on for the afternoon. They used to say to me
that up north I must have needed to eat lots of potatoes,
milky pasta, bread. I didn't. I needed the thing
in the air that makes the batter rise.

Cambium

Soon I was told that pine scent to the air was neither the living forest nor green. Rather, a song in sap: *now and at the hour,* acres of stump, ringed discs the colour of quick. The thousand flat moons of a sky. The elegy would be over by morning, the air less pungent cool, and the sun baking the sap-salve dry.

This as I held a gun in my hands, the pad of my finger at rest on the trigger's tiny, curving bow. What I hadn't expected: desire. It would take so little. An imperceptible movement in my wrist, the smallest give to release a breath and trace an unknown trajectory.

All along I must have been waiting. One blind shot, and for once, proof could be brought back to me: whether I had been alone. I have always supposed that what proves faith is a wound. The blood's rich red; the darkness, leaking sap.

Poem for One Raccoon

Elegance of wearing nothing but white.
A shade clearer than sand, the opacity
of sliced starfruit they served for breakfast.
A taste barely there and just beyond
the French doors, the golf-green palms
submitting to the breeze, the cove was blue
as my iris, eye of the storm in quiet.
That weekend I was his kept woman.
So when he touched my white sleeve
I didn't know, anymore, whether I could turn away.

Driving inland on Sunday, we hit a *mapache*
stunned by our headlights. That word
was a body left behind without shape
or translation, a gloss in a porous rut
of the ocean road. Back door of language.
As the waves gave us up to punitive silence,
I scanned the black highway, hoping
it would give me something for the name.

Water Born

I.

I wonder. Can one trust a voice? If one will trust
what can be thrown, and lost, and changed.

You said water borne but I heard water born.
So we were talking about origins, the filling of lungs.

The chest cavernous, shortness of breath. Even the flies
tired, the last one doped in the fold of your pant leg.

To accept without proof. Is there such a great difference
between assumption and belief? To be thirsty, to have thirst.

Water boils at lower temperatures further from sea level.
I hear this as impatience; as a homesickness.

II.

Muscle memory is selective too. We set out, stunned feet,
cross the river. It is one finger, a caress at the ankle bone.

Clear water, clear as the voice that called your name
beneath the window, the night your restlessness answered it.

The air so thin we could have articulated anything.
So: *I can't sleep*. The words have their clarity.

River under rock, meandering, doubling back.
Water will find the simplest route downwards.

Here. An arrival that asks to be pronounced.
Do you believe this? A wavering: your voice, the river.

Mate de Coca
(Cuzco, Peru)

No, it's not enough, momentary
in the throat. This threadbare air,
this one breath,
         twelve steps
to the terraza, one breath
      stretched over the Andes,
harsh, red shadow.

Blood pales in the absence
of oxygen, blue veins, blue lips, blue-
grey sun on the wall. And warmth
can't penetrate stone.

Weakness is a cup
that has cooled between my palms
because I couldn't raise it to my lips.

Not that the strength wasn't
in my muscles, but that it wasn't in me:
my hands are being warmed.
It didn't occur to me to drink.

Leaves from the dry sides of hills
settle in my cup. And they have sent a boy
with wind-raw cheeks who reminds me
when to hunger.
           When I hear him.

The brittle leaves soak, and steep.

And because I believe in what
     I'm short of,
I believe in breath.

The Last Syllable of Recorded Time

not one sound fears the silence
that extinguishes it
— John Cage

The echo as captivity, and sound
confined by the Andina range
finds shape. Chords suspend

every name. In such a valley
the tide would have no words
for your language: its tongue

cleft between low and high.
To speak is leaning into wind,
your scribe and the wave's

undercurrent. The last syllable
records time: you have the night
strobe of fireflies, refracting

prism of your voice, the caul
of mist and throat. Each shift
you've heard has been music, or,

cry out again. You fear the sound
that extinguishes. Solitude
is your own voice

against your cheek, waves
siphoned through wire:
I would have called, but —

Wind-over-Wave

... when we arrived in town, I explained to her that this
could never be, that city life was not what she had thought it
was in all her naivety of a wave who had never left the sea.
— Octavio Paz

This won't be entirely clear.
It's so easy to forget the body
is water, water changed,
that old party trick.

How does one mark the first day
of return? I've come from seasonless
to shock-spring, to the inconstant
month of March — it's 24° above zero
in the North Saskatchewan's valley
and the snow still reaches
to my knees. The cliffs are loud
with runoff, an authority — here,
the convections are so deliberate
I split two currents: warm, cool,
they cut across my body in a wave,
imperfect curve, the way I sliced
the grapefruit one morning and you said,
"She is not good at straight lines."

Now, I can't measure this winter
in terms of the one before.
Carving the city, the belt of bare aspen
and new mud shelters a weather
that feigns independence — from us,
from the westerlies, and ocean currents
named for children; el niño, la niña,

boy-child, girl-child, storm,
drought, wind-over-wave.

It's getting too warm.
But the ravine unwelcomes wind
and sunlight, and transition
seems so temporary. One might believe
winter's thrown down its parka
for no other reason than joy.
The season flips and equivocates:
the equinox is just a night
in praise of equilibrium.

From areas of high concentration
to areas of lower. Water
as charity, as the body
yearning for stasis.
At the poles, it's salt that
incites the current — as water
gives to the air, salt gains
in density, plunges to depths where
the ocean shows its age and moves
slowly. During the last ice age
fresh water was bound up
with cold, and salt swarmed
the oceans more freely.
Currents were strong, stronger.

The body approaches the ocean
through the blood: its salinity
equal to the salinity of the sea.

The membrane is permeable:
Allow the bearer to pass freely
without let or hindrance.
Before I left the prairies
I knew the ocean was salt water
but I didn't know how it gets in your eyes.
Or how it takes your weight away.
Aqueous, crystalline, doesn't matter.
It stings like sweat in the wind-burned
cracks of the hands, draws water
from your body as a chinook
parches the skin.

Hydration is balance.
Thirst can't be quenched
on water alone — too much dilutes the body.
And salt can make you buoyant
or it can make you weak.
Trouble is, its lack isn't revealed
through craving, though I've heard
islanders who move inland
feel a constant thirst. Salt
and loss: on this first day
as I run the ravine, what's left me
can be seen on my face, cheeks
traced with the minerals
water leaves behind. To pass
without let, or hindrance...

Transience of water,
the changeling. Winds
over waves, over my body —
the air is cooler now and
where water evaporates, I feel
the small robbery of heat.
My skin's warmth chosen
for the drop's rapture, kiss
of a phase change.

A return — is this spring?
The season begins here
as white air trapped in ice.
You crack it open
with your heel, that's reason enough
to break your stride.

Part III

Translator's Note

Any errors or inadequacies are solely the responsibility of
the translator.

I suppose it is also the responsibility
of the translator to confess:
these poems were not translated
with the assistance and/or permission
of the author. To be honest
even the book is stolen, I picked it up
over dinner while my host distracted
his wife — unexpectedly arrived —
when he returned, he threw salt
over his left shoulder and raised his fingers
to his head affecting horns: '*mi diablita*,'
he said, though this word did not appear
in my dictionary and his charade did nothing
but increase my general confusion.
I should also mention I have not been intimate
with the poet's work, this being
in fact the only poem I've read
(the book is long and falls naturally open);
in addition I did not directly follow
the eight stages of translation
but rather skipped to the final chapter,
"Attuning the Ear to Cultural Nuance,"
so I thought it prudent to assess
the context of the scene,
the large grains of salt and surprising
sweetness of melted cream, hence

the breaks in syntax, the subject-
object inversion and additions of
personal pronouns (tradutorre traditore).
I was only assisted by a second-
hand phrasebook and hardly
speak the language, but in my defence I didn't
even know he was married.

The Word According to Hernán Cortés

To begin with thirst.
A clear sea, limestone depths.
Then arrival
by the grin of the moon.

That morning (God, I was thirsty)
I wet my fingers
in the fused stamen of hibiscus.
To twine in her hair, for what else
is conquest?

I find testament in all places.
For now, a catalogue of prophecy:
shattered comets, lunar eclipse.
Details of savagery.

Could you think me ungrateful?
Golden shores braided
with silver, and a land
that keeps me honest?
I say: I have
come to serve God
and His Majesty, and also
to get riches.

I leave translation up to God.
Divine simplicity.

To ask, and receive.
The messenger arrived
at last with fresh water,

with gold and daughters.
He broke the knobbed skin
of a cactus pear, stained
his fingers red. Our breakfast,
I presume; he said, *Take, eat.*

Horse Latitudes of the Atlantic
(Malinche Travels Home)

Days the greatest weakness
is the wind, and we cannot
be light enough. We eat meat,
stilled muscle, pare the ship
to ribs. Morning is what we ask
our bodies to consume.

Belt of calms.
With a lens held to the sun,
I sear a pin of white gold
to my palm. Because reason
is meagre, boredom a cruel governor
of men. The moon changes shape
without falling from the horizon, myth
of proximity, the salt burn of lack
and sleep.

Stagnant astride the held breath
of the sea. They say, Marina,
what might you offer, for wind?
I could tell them it is easier
to drive in a gasp than force
its release.

My hand in the last earth-cool
store of coffee beans. To dim
this migraine of heat. My hair shorn
(mats of salt, my swollen
tongue) and seven weeks
for a blood blister to heal.

To fill a sail: surrender. Exhale
the same morning as the rough
bundle of burlap disappears
underwater. The rust colt
I folded in canvas, his eyes the milk
blue of having never seen the sun.

Teosinte

Many are deliberating the ancestry of corn.
One man has chosen to hold out his thumb
so that we might all consider the centuries
that had been spent waiting for the first ear
to reach that size. Then at last all its sexual organs
turned female and it was saved from itself
by husbandry, like mothers, drawn out of caves
bearing baskets of maize. It is true
that our best stories are apocryphal.
After his years away, they asked Cortés,
What is Mexico like? He tore a page from the book
that lay open on the table, crumpled it in his fist
and dropped it to the ground: It's like this.

Twenty Thousand Mirrors and the Monarch Migration

Your exodus: a synchronized
direction of the sun.
For one day, in our hands.
Caught in all manner of metals:
small mirrors, silver pendants,
from corrugated tin on the hills
to the wide belly of your plane.
To say there has been no shortage
of love. A pyramid of sun.

But we are not strangers
to departure. When the earth tilts
there will be another migration,
harvest of fruit, to bring home
a portion. There was a time
when all that was asked
was the sacrifice of a butterfly.
The only stain the iridescence
of its wings on their fingers.

I left that same day, the farewell
also mine. The reflected sun
and a moment when I believed
love could be earned.
A jetstream circling the city,
your extra revolution in the sky.
And a monarch sunrise, orange light
spilling over these mountains
like morning, like roses from a cloak.

Immaculate Hologram

No need for clocks we have the rain.
We have a city contingent on buses,
the buses have a schedule: it is imperceptible.
We will be re-ordering what is random.
Buses random. Rain precise.

An incision of rain. The same metrical violence
of an hour, only liquid. This time yesterday,
a woman drowned driving home
across Lopez Mateos. The street was dry
by morning: I know, I didn't believe it either.

I've heard turkeys drown in the rain.
They look up to see what's on their heads,
their long throats fill. It doesn't look good for me.
For years I could read words, not clocks,
and the gutter is climbing to my knees.

In Guadalajara the bus stop is an abstract place.
The bus in motion will continue in motion,
it will displace its own weight in water.
Men dangle out the doors with no visible hold,
calling ¡Guerita! they reach me through rain.

This is how the Virgin appeared to me:
in the confine of humidity, the passengers' teeth
luminous in the black light. A hologram decal,
décalage of time — an hour collapsed at the window
and this rain with its arbitrary logic.

Upon Running into a Supposedly Dead Revolutionary, after Having Written His Elegy

I know now why
I've always hated to travel.
Diesel thins the blood
and any ache you've supported
hollows out. This is how it is:
your head in your hands
for days. Nothing
as you had once believed.

I blamed my last lost
letter on the donkey's broken leg.
There could have been a correlation.
The donkey wheezed into the afternoon
and hobbled about the plaza,
its knee a crooked knob
halfway akimbo.
The donkey was paid relatively
little notice. Its scream
was like asphyxiation,
it drew out all other air and sound.

Burrito means little donkey.
I assumed in my ignorance this
was the cultural equivalent to pigs-in-a-blanket.

It turned out I had only discovered the literal
translation of the Spanish diminutive.

cubita: rum & coke in a blanket
guërita: blonde in a blanket
tempranito: very early in a blanket

So tempranito, in Barcelona, Paz
might hardly have been surprised by you,
though I assume he had believed
in your death among other things.
Elegía a un compañero muerto —
circumstance did not render the poem
obsolete for long.

Instante vertiginoso:
the point of intersection
between two times and two spaces.

When I saw the one
to whom I had not written,
it was as if all the little bulls of Pamplona
had stopped running.

Me voy a mi casa porque no entiendo
nada de lo que ocurre...

I am going home
because I do not understand.

Cartografía

Antonio Deltoro

(a Dámaso Alonso, cartógrafo de las palabras)

Diques invisibles para las palabras.
Lineas que sin serlo nos dividen.
En la claridad de un mapa
de colores distintos, están pintadas
las distintas familias de palabras.
Un hombre y una mujer se miran,
se hablan: no se entienden.
¿Se sueña distinto, más tenue,
en inglés que en español?
¿Las neblinas nórdicas, el azul de la montaña
se mezclan con el idioma?
De cuando en cuando una palabra
cruza su frontera,
se arriesga por despeñaderos, por falanges
de palabras enemigas, se casa con otra
que hospitalaria la recibe, la declina
o le sirve como escudo,
poco a poco las palabras se vuelven
mestizas, se acriollan;
a aquella familia de palabras morenas
le sale una hija rubia,
a aquella otra una con los ojos azules,
poco a poco por ellos van entrando
nubes sutiles de paisajes nórdicos
a tierras tropicales;
guijarros, humedades de mar,
a escarpados picos,
sensuales pensamientos de muchachas
a frentes adustas y otoñales.

Cartography

Antonio Deltoro
(for Dámaso Alonso, cartographer of words)

Invisible dikes for words.
Lines that don't exist divide us.
On a map there is clarity:
distinct families of words
are painted distinct colours.
A man and a woman look at each other,
speak at each other: neither is understood.
Does one dream differently, more faintly,
in English than in Spanish?
Does nordic mist, the blue of the mountains
intermingle with the language?
Now and then a word
crosses the border,
braves cliffs, phalanxes
of enemy words. It marries another,
one who welcomes it, and declines
or serves as a shield.
Little by little these words turn
mestiza, become creole;
this family of dark-complexioned words
will have one blonde daughter;
another, a blue-eyed girl.
Through them, little by little
subtle clouds of nordic landscapes
carry into tropical lands;
pebbles and the humid ocean air
blow toward steep peaks,
the sensual thoughts of girls
with stern, autumnal foreheads.

Las palabras erosionan acantilados,
arenillas del desierto van destiñendo
con ellas marcados rasgos.
Las palabras castellanas se desbroncan.
En silencio las palabras se aman
cuando se encuentran gentes de distinto idioma.
Hay palabras que no se dejan conquistar
y acaban.
Pero las palabras aptas, las jóvenes, vencen su pudor,
su timidez, su hosquedad adolescente
y al fin se aman, se entienden,
porque para la palabra no hay nada extranjero.

Words erode escarpments,
shift desert sands and cause
remarkable features to fade.
Castilian words calm their anger.
When people of different languages meet,
words are making love in silence.
Some words resist seduction
and disappear.
But the clever words, the young ones, overcome
their modesty, shyness and adolescent hostility,
. and at last fall in love, understanding one.another,
because to the word nothing is really foreign.

Secondary Sources

I.

Every written language encounters
its limit in the effort of transcription.
When the conquistadores wrote home with the word
for *corn*, the name of this
or that blue valley, they turned phonemes
they could not even really hear
Castilian, imagined diphthongs
and the iconic X. The ear says
I will go to a new world now,
but it is a weak missionary.
Easily disoriented, seasick often.

II.

In pain, all lands are charted
in degrees of hot and cold.
Every movement is the final departure, the *yes,*
my love, I'll write, from the illiterate
young sailor of the Santa Inés,
and such was his excitement, he meant it.
But the Roman alphabet was as constant
in its enigma as the Mayan glyphs.
Ships were burned at harbour
so there would be no question of returning home.
The first and last time he held a pen
was to sign his name, *X.*

III.

And afterwards, the memory
mutes but does not disappear.
Despite the Conquest and every invasion before,
the toponymy of the Mayan territories
remains unchanged. In Oaxaca,
a man breaks his wrist and cries out —
not in the adopted language
he's been speaking most of his life,
but from within, in the clarity
before feeling anything at all, the tongue
he thought he'd lost.

Milagro por el nevado in Three Translations

I. Prayer to la nevada

For speech, a milagro
the shape of a tongue.
Silver, for words,
for their mercurial flow.

What will you do with those?
What will you bring, what prayer
can you hold in your fist?
Begin counting. I have found

flint stones like paired kidneys.
Tin raindrops, breasts for want
of milk and hearts of stamped nickel.
Along the ridge, the sun caught

on a dangling navel, glanced
off small ears. These hieroglyphs
of prayer. The cipher is simple,
when it rains: listen. The sound

of skirts plaited with bangles.
Another pilgrimage: charms
strung with brass pins, gathering
the blue folds of the Sierra Madre.

II. Milagro por el nevado

Para el habla, un milagro
parecido a la lengua.
Plateado, como palabra,
como la fluidez mercurial.

¿Qué harás con ellas?
¿Qué vas a traer, cuál oración
puedes agarrar en el puño?
Empieza a contar. He encontrado

pedernal en la forma de dos riñones.
Gotas estañadas, pechos por la falta
de leche y corazones de níquel marcado.
Por la cordillera, el sol atrapado

por un ombligo colgado, reboteado
contra orejitas. Estos jeroglíficos
de rezar. La cifra es sencilla,
cuando llueve: escucha. Suena

a faldas trenzadas de esclavas.
Otra peregrinación: amuletos encordados
con imperdibles de latón, reuniendo
los dobles azules de la Sierra Madre.

III.   Miracle from the snowpeak

Passing for speech, a miracle
that seems like language.
A plated word, glossed
with the fluency of mercury.

What will you make with them?
What will you bring, which sentence
can you grab with your fist?
Now for the story. I have found

kidney-shaped fragments of documents.
Drops on tin, courage that lacks only
milk and sweethearts punched from coins.
The volcanic vertebrae, the sun taken

by an umbilical cord, ricocheted
these glyphs against its inner ear
to pray. The numeral is innocent,
when it rains: listen. The striking clock

at the foot of the mountain, braided
with slaves and other travellers: ropes
of amulets, the unloseable brass, reuniting
the blue doubles of the mothering range.

Goodnight, Cow Jumping

> I suppose hearing a language is a different way of feeling
> the words. I don't suppose there are synonyms really.
> I wonder if moon means exactly the same thing as luna.
> — Jorge Luis Borges

You could always ask who
is held captive there. Man,
or the shadow of a rabbit caught
mid-leap. Call this linguistics
of the dark seas: maria.

Or try empirical evidence.
Compare the crescent moon,
fingernail quick, a sliver
shaved over Venus,
with la luna creciente, growing
grin over Mexico.

Why not ask lovers,
for who else knows as much
about moonlight? Claro de luna,
clarity of moon. La luna is a guitar
beneath your window, gallo,
which translates as rooster
and means serenade.

There's our lovers' moon,
the harvest, red disc at rest
on the prairie horizon.
Or the honeymoon, née
hymeneal moon; not quite
la luna de miel, sticky
bee-yellow light.

Each phase finds another
lunulate discord. Once in a blue —
you hear the luna moon. Batting
towards light, elliptical; language
like the shadow of a body
thrown by a lamp. Mouth
what little you understand.

Notes on the Poems

The epigraph to "The Red Belt" by Friedrich Nietzsche is from *Thus Spake Zarathustra*, trans. Thomas Common. (New York: Random House, 1982).

All but the final lines of "The Good Hostess" are taken from *The Joy of Cooking* by Irma S. Rombauer and Marion Rombauer Becker (New York: Signet, 1974).

The epigraph to "The Last Syllable of Recorded Time" by John Cage is from *Silence: Lectures and Writings* (Middletown, Conn: Wesleyan UP, 1961). The title of the poem is from *Macbeth*.

The epigraph to "Wind-over-Wave" by Octavio Paz is from "My Life with the Wave," *Aguila o Sol* (México: Fondo de Cultura Económica, 1973), my translation.

"Horse Latitudes of the Atlantic" imagines the return of Malinche (also known as Marina) to Mexico after a period of time spent in Spain. Malinche was an Aztec woman taken as mistress by Cortés upon his arrival. Her assistance as an interpreter facilitated Cortes's conquest of Mexico.

"Twenty Thousand Mirrors and the Monarch Migration" is a response to Pope John Paul II's visit to Mexico City in 1999. As he departed, people waited in the streets with mirrors to signal their good-bye.

The final italicized lines of "Upon Running into a Supposedly Dead Revolutionary" are taken from *Itinerario* by Octavio Paz (México: Fondo de Cultura Económica, 1993). Paz wrote the poem "Elegía a un compañero muerto en el frente de Aragón" for his friend José Bosch, whom he later ran into in Barcelona.

"The Rooster on the Balcony" is a translation of the poem by Elva Macías, *Círculo del Sueño* (México: Literature Joven, 1975). It is reprinted and translated with the permission of Elva Macías.

"Cartografía" by Antonio Deltoro was originally published in *Poesía Reunida* (México: UNAM, 1999). It is reprinted and translated by permission of Antonio Deltoro.

The poems included in "Milagro por la nevada" are original. "Prayer to la nevada" was written in English and then translated into Spanish. The final poem is the English translation of the Spanish version. A milagro (miracle) is a small charm that is pinned to the dress of the Virgin, symbolic of a prayer.

Acknowledgements

A number of these poems have appeared in the following journals:
*The Antigonish Review, Arc, CV2, Event, The Fiddlehead, Grain,
The Malahat Review, Prairie Fire,* and *Prism International.* I thank
the editors for including my work.

I am grateful for financial assistance from both the Alberta
Foundation for the Arts and the Banff Centre. I also thank the
people at Goose Lane for their time and attention.

Lisa Martin-DeMoor has provided great insight and friendship
during the writing of these poems. So have James Langer and
Vanessa Moeller: thank you. For editorial revelations, I thank
my editor Marlene Cookshaw, Ross Leckie, Don McKay and Stan
Dragland. For early and continuing encouragement, I thank Ruth
Powell, Olga Costopoulos and Bert Almon.

I wish to thank Antonio Deltoro and Elva Macías for generously
allowing me to publish translations of their work.

A special note of thanks goes to my family, who provide me with
love and support, and to Adam Dickinson for sharing it all.